FRANKLIN PARK PUBLIC LIBRARY
FRANKLIN PARK, IL.

Lady Bird Johnson

Anita Yasuda

WEIGL PUBLISHERS INC.
"Creating Inspired Learning"
www.weigl.com

Published by Weigl Publishers Inc.
350 5th Avenue, 59th Floor
New York, NY 10118
Website: www.weigl.com

Library of Congress Cataloging-in-Publication Data

Yasuda, Anita.
 Lady Bird Johnson : my life / Anita Yasuda.
    p. cm.
 Includes index.
 ISBN 978-1-61690-062-5 (alk. paper) -- ISBN 978-1-61690-063-2 (softcover : alk. paper) --
 ISBN 978-1-61690-064-9 (e-book)
 1. Johnson, Lady Bird, 1912-2007--Juvenile literature. 2. Johnson, Lyndon B. (Lyndon Baines), 1908-1973--Juvenile literature.
 3. Presidents' spouses--United States--Biography--Juvenile literature. I. Title.
 E848.J64Y37 2010
 973.923092--dc22
 [B]
                              2010005476

Printed in the United States of America in North Mankato, Minnesota
1 2 3 4 5 6 7 8 9 0 14 13 12 11 10

042010
WEP264000

Editor: Heather C. Hudak   **Design**: Kenzie Browne

All of the Internet URLs given in the book were valid at the time of publication. However, due to the dynamic nature of the Internet, some addresses may have changed, or sites may have ceased to exist since publication. While the author and publisher regret any inconvenience this may cause readers, no responsibility for any such changes can be accepted by either the author or the publisher.

Every reasonable effort has been made to trace ownership and to obtain permission to reprint copyright material. The publishers would be pleased to have any errors or omissions brought to their attention so that they may be corrected in subsequent printings.

Weigl acknowledges Getty Images and the LBJ Library as the primary image suppliers for this title.

CONTENTS

Who is Lady Bird Johnson?

Claudia "Lady Bird" Johnson was first lady to the 36th president of the United States. Her husband was President Lyndon B. Johnson. Johnson is remembered for her love of nature and her work to keep the United States beautiful.

As first lady, Johnson cleaned up the **capital**. She had flowers and trees planted. Then, she worked to have trash cleaned from roadsides and highways.

Lady Bird and Lyndon were engaged to be married only seven weeks after their first date.

5

Growing Up

Claudia Alta Taylor was born in Texas on December 22, 1912. Her nickname, "Lady Bird," was given to her by a family nanny.

Johnson was the third child born to Minnie and Thomas Taylor. She had two older brothers. The family lived in a big home called "The Brick House." Johnson's father had a cotton business and two general stores. A sign above one of his stores read "Dealer in Everything."

All About Texas

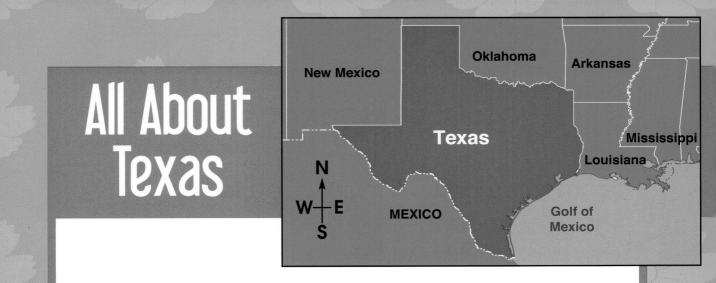

- Texas became the 28th state on December 29, 1845.
- Austin is the capital of Texas.
- There are 5,000 types of wildflowers in Texas.
- The state flower is the bluebonnet.
- Lady Bird Lake flows through downtown Austin.

The state flag of Texas is called the "Lone Star Flag." It was **adopted** in 1845.

Influences

Johnson's mother, Minnie, loved to read. She often read to her children. Learning was important to Minnie.

Minnie died when Johnson was five years old. Johnson went to work with her father. She played at the store and slept upstairs.

Johnson's Aunt Effie came to look after her. Effie taught her to love books. She showed Johnson the beauty of nature. They walked in the pine woods and listened to the birds.

9

Practice Makes Perfect

Johnson went to a one-room schoolhouse. In the summers, she visited family in Alabama. At age 15, Johnson went to a girls' school in Dallas. She was a good student and had many colleges to choose from. In 1930, Johnson went to the University of Texas in Austin. She studied history and journalism.

Johnson was the only first lady to build her own wealth. In 1942, she bought a radio station. Johnson worked hard to make it succeed. She hired staff and even cleaned floors at times.

Key Events

Lady Bird met Lyndon B. Johnson in Austin, Texas. He worked for a **congressman**. Lady Bird and Lyndon married in 1934. They had two daughters, Lynda Bird and Luci Baines. The family lived in Washington, D.C. In 1937, Lyndon ran for Congress.

When Lyndon served in World War II, Lady Bird ran his congressional office. She helped the people he represented.

In 1964, Lyndon ran for president. Johnson **campaigned** on her own to help him win the election. It was the first time a president's wife did this. After Lyndon won the race, Lady Bird helped with government programs. One program was called **Project Head Start**.

In 1972, the Johnsons gave their Texas ranch to the people of the United States. It became a national historic site.

13

Overcoming Obstacles

Effie tried to look after Johnson when she was young, but Effie was not well herself. Johnson had to learn to take care of herself.

Johnson went on a train trip to talk to people about **civil rights**. Her train was called the *Lady Bird Special*. Some people disagreed with what Johnson had to say. They yelled at her, but she did not back down from her beliefs.

By the end of her train trip, Lady Bird had given 47 speeches. About 500,000 people heard her speak.

Lady Bird Special

15

Achievements and Successes

Johnson enjoyed the outdoors. It shaped the way she saw the world. Johnson believed that cleaning up the outdoors would make the nation a better place.

To help protect nature, Johnson formed a special group. It was called the Committee for a More Beautiful Capital. The group cleaned up neighborhoods in the city and planted flowers and trees.

Johnson's work stretched across the nation. She showed people the beauty of the country by hiking in **redwood** forests and visiting national parks.

In 1965, Johnson's work inspired a **bill** to cut down on highway **billboards** and litter. It was nicknamed "Lady Bird's Bill."

In 1970, Johnson published a book about the time she spent at the White House. It was called *A White House Diary*.

In 1977, Johnson was awarded the Presidential Medal of Freedom. This is the highest honor that a person who is not a soldier can receive.

Johnson kept working after leaving the White House. In 1982, she set up a center in Austin for **native** plants. It is called the Lady Bird Johnson Wildflower Center.

What is a First Lady?

Harriet Lane was the first woman to be called "first lady." She was President Buchanan's niece. Lane was the hostess at White House events. Today, the president's wife takes on the role of first lady.

The first lady's main role is to be the hostess of the White House. She entertains politicians from around the world. The first lady also tours the world as a **goodwill ambassador**. She supports many causes.

First Ladies Through History

Like Johnson, these first ladies have played an important role in history.

Martha Washington

Washington was born in Virginia. She married George Washington in 1759. In 1902, her picture was used on a U.S. postage stamp.

Dolley Madison

Madison married James Madison in 1794. She was the first first lady to officially have a project that helped the public. She founded a home for orphaned girls.

Jacqueline Kennedy Onassis

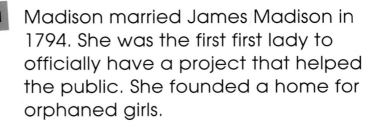

Kennedy Onassis married John F. Kennedy in 1953. Kennedy Onassis created the White House Historical Association. This group promotes the history of the White House.

Timeline

1912 | Claudia Alta Taylor was born on December 22 near Karnack, Texas.

1934 | Johnson graduates from the University of Texas. She marries Lyndon B. Johnson.

1941–1942 | Johnson maintains her husband's congressional office while he is at war.

1963 | Johnson becomes first lady.

1964 | Johnson promotes Project Head Start.

1965	Johnson begins programs to clean up communities.
1971	The Lyndon Baines Johnson Library opens at the University of Texas.
1982	The National Wildflower Research Center in Austin is created.
1988	Johnson accepts a **Congressional Gold Medal** for her work. She writes a best-selling book, *Wildflowers Across America*, with Carlton Lees.
1997	The National Wildflower Research Center is renamed the Lady Bird Johnson Wildflower Center.
2007	Johnson dies in her home on July 11.

Write a Biography

A person's life story can be the subject of a book. This kind of book is called a biography. Biographies describe the lives of people who have had great success or done important things to help others. These people may be alive today, or they may have lived many years ago.

Try writing your own biography. First, decide who you want to write about. You can choose a first lady, such as Lady Bird Johnson, or any other person you find interesting. Then, find out if your library has any books about this person.

Write down the key events in this person's life.

- What was this person's childhood like?
- What has he or she accomplished?
- What are his or her goals?
- What makes this person special or unusual?

Answer the questions in your notebook. Your answers will help you write your biography review.

Find Out More

To learn more about Lady Bird Johnson, visit these websites.

Information about all of the first ladies can be found at the official White House First Ladies website.
www.whitehouse.gov/about/first-ladies

Learn more about Lady Bird Johnson at this site.
www.pbs.org/ladybird

The Lyndon Baines Johnson Library and Museum website has information and pictures of the Johnson family.
www.lbjlib.utexas.edu

Visit the Lady Bird Johnson Wildflower Center website.
www.wildflower.org

Glossary

adopted: officially approved

bill: a new law that has not yet been approved

billboards: large signs on the side of roadways

campaigned: took part in activities to help achieve a goal, such as giving speeches to win an election

capital: the place where the national government works

civil rights: the rights of all people to freedom and equal treatment

Congressional Gold Medal: one of the highest honors a person can receive; given to a person who performs an outstanding act

congressman: a person who is a member of the national government

goodwill ambassador: a representative of a country who travels to another country

native: to naturally live in an area

Project Head Start: a preschool program for children in need

redwood: a very tall type of tree that grows in California

Index